AROUND
GLOUCESTER
IN OLD PHOTOGRAPHS

SOUTHGATE STREET AND THE BELL HOTEL 1925. Most of the Bell was demolished in the 1970s to make way for the Southgate Street entrance to Woolworths, now a branch of Marks and Spencers. The 16th century part, the Berkeley family's Gloucester town house remained intact and is now all that remains of this once famous posting house, or, at least took the name of the old posting house. The author Henry Fielding was obviously acquainted with Gloucester and the Bell features in Tom Jones, published in 1749.

... Being arrived here they (Tom Jones, and Partridge his servant) chose for their house of entertainment the sign of the Bell, an excellent house indeed, and which I do most seriously recommend to every reader who shall visit this ancient city. The master of it is brother to the great preacher Whitefield; but is absolutely untainted with the pernicious principles of methodism ...

George Whitefield was only 35 years old when this was published, and making his mark. Fielding was very much for the established church, and not afraid of punchy political or religious barbs.

AROUND
GLOUCESTER
IN OLD PHOTOGRAPHS

COLLECTED BY
ALAN SUTTON

ALAN SUTTON
1987

Alan Sutton Publishing Limited
Brunswick Road · Gloucester

First published 1987

British Library Cataloguing in Publication Data

Around Gloucester in old photographs
1. Gloucester (Gloucestershire)—History
I. Sutton, Alan, *1949–*
942.4'14   DA690.G5

ISBN 0-806299-400-4

Typesetting and origination by
Alan Sutton Publishing Limited.
Printed in Great Britain by
WBC Print Limited · Bristol.

CONTENTS

TO MELINDA

AERIAL VIEW OF THE CITY, c.1960

INTRODUCTION

In 1734 Samuel and Nathaniel Buck published their views of Gloucester; the most famous of which is The North West Prospect of the City of Gloucester which shows the city as if viewed by a low flying pilot from a position somewhere between Over and Maisemore. In this view it can be seen that the city boasted at least two windmills. The glass house can be seen in its full conical splendour (see page 15) and the tower of Holy Trinity Church can be seen in the middle of Westgate Street. Between the cathedral and Westgate, fine formal gardens are fronting on to the river, and many trows can be seen moored up on the river quay – ninety years before the docks were built. Obviously the Buck brothers could not hire a helicopter and take a photograph on which to base their engraving, but much of what was engraved could be seen from the ground, and the only requirement was a slight adjustment to the perspective. The Buck brothers' accuracy is known to be good from engravings in other parts of the country where much that they delineated still stands, but even so, some licence must have crept into their work and cannot be compared to a photograph. Would it not be marvellous to have a good photograph of the city in 1734 – or better still a complete book of them! That would have shown us our great-(seven times)-grandparents and the Gloucester that they knew. No doubt the city had narrow dirty streets, and the smell would have been intolerable to our refined senses – our ancestors had little choice without piped water or sewers. To give a small example of an inn in Northgate Street just a few years after our date take the following advertisement of 10 January 1744.

Notice is hereby given

That the Inn, called the Black Spread-Eagle, in the Lower Northgate-Street, Gloucester, is now kept by Thomas and Sarah Cole, where all Gentlemen and Others may depend on civil Usage and good Entertainment.

N.B. There is Stabling for above an hundred Horses, and a large Yard stock'd with Coal for the Use of the Hill-Country Waggons, and a Parcel of very fine Hay with the Stables; and at Lady-Day next there will be fine Grazing Grounds for Depasturing Welch Cattle in their way to London.

This inn would have been on the very edge of the city, with fields just beyond. The city as a whole would have been compact and densely populated; with narrow lanes and crowded tenements.

It is difficult to visualise how Gloucester must have looked at this time. Many buildings standing today were in existence then; but the context in which they exist today is totally different from that of 250 years ago. A fine timbered house may have had ancient and decrepit tenements on each side. These tenements may have been replaced with brick buildings, and even these brick buidlings may now have gone – to be replaced by a plague of the ubiquitous building societies! The fine timber building may still stand, but its neighbours may now look a little incongruous. This image of the Gloucester in 1734 is difficult to visualise in full. By what gauge or yardstick can we form the mental picture? From period programmes on television or from visits to museums? Photographs are just not available to assist us.

Our descendants will be more lucky in their jogging back in history to a comparable time span of 250 years. A photographic archive will show them how the city looked, and which buildings stood on which sites.

Readers aged between 30 and upwards have witnessed a unique experience. More change has occurred in the last twenty years than perhaps over the previous 150 years, and this book well illustrates the changing city. For those aged twenty or below, California Crossing will mean nothing at all. Long traffic jams at the Barton Gates will not be part of their personal recollections. For those aged 30 or below the thought of cattle being herded into what is now the bus station will seem most amusing. And yet Gloucester like any other town or city has always experienced the slow but constant metamorphosis, it is just that this change is now accelerating at quite an alarming pace, with not all of the change being for the better. Happily for posterity and future generations who wish to peep back at us we have the benefit of photography. A photograph cannot show how we lived, but it shows how we looked, the exterior environment, and throws out clues of day to day life styles.

This book shows a selection of photographic views from the 1870s through to the 1950s. I have tried to avoid repetitions from Jill Voyce's excellent book *Gloucester in Old Photographs*, and I have attempted to widen the area, bringing in pictures from the suburbs and surrounding villages. Hopefully this book will be a success and generate further similar publications, which may include even more views from the periphery of the city. If any reader owns an interesting picture, please do send it in to me at the Brunswick Road address for consideration in a future volume.

Alan Sutton
Hydefield
Uley
Gloucestershire

MOUNT STREET c.1880. This is one of my favourite photographs in this book. The subjects are of a class that were rarely photographed although they made up the largest proportion of the population. The large lady in the centre rather reminds me of the washerwoman in Kenneth Graham's *Wind in the Willows*. Two of the children were too impatient to last out the twenty seconds or so that this exposure would have taken, and for posterity they have left a blur. The church centre background is St. Mary de Lode.

The River and the Docks

SEVERNSIDE CHARACTERS c.1905. A lovely photograph of lovelies! Probably taken at Stonebench, the occasion is unknown. The character front left seems rather incongruous amongst the rest, obviously a flamboyant who was determined not to let the occasion pass without his mark.

THE BARGE SUNRISEN in East Channel, 27 January 1940. Her captain was Walter Butt.

SPARTAN, GLOSTER C. 1900. This marvellous picture is an enlargement of the view shown on page 25.

THE QUAY C.1906. Ferryman on the east bank, Castle Meads shown on the west. The round building shown centre is the old glass house shown in detail on page 15 and described in the introduction.

GLOUCESTER PRISON c.1906. The same ferryman is this time on the west bank, the photographer is looking east towards the city and the prison.

THE OLD GLASSHOUSE c.1930. This strangely shaped building was originally much taller when built at the end of the seventeenth century as a glass making furnace. See the engraving on page 8. The building was unfortunately demolished in August 1933.

THE QUAYSIDE, RIVER LOCK AND DOCKS IN 1906. Again, our same ferryman, this time once more on the east bank. This ferryman may be Henry Bubb who was forced in October 1906 to ferry five escaped convicts to Castle Meads.

The prison was built between 1787 and 1792 to replace the notorious old prison built out of the ruins of Gloucester Castle. Life for prisoners in the un-reformed prison was hard. In John Howard's book *The State of the Prisons* first published in 1777, he reports that at Gloucester he found twenty fines (detained for pecuniary penalties unsatisfied) who were half naked and almost famished as they did not qualify for the county allowance. Three months later when he saw them again they were in better state of health due to the philanthropy of Robert Raikes.

Prisoners were allowed to charge new arrivals garnish of one shilling and sixpence. This was a custom prevalent in many prisons by which newcomers were forced to pay a forfeit for a round of drinks on pain of losing all their clothes in default! Prisoners had to pay for their food, if they could not they may well starve. Howard further noted there was no proper separation of women which resulted in 'licentious intercourse of the sexes', that five or six children had recently been born in the prison and that death from smallpox and gaol fever were common events.

THE KETCH SABRINA C.1900. The ketch was built at Samuel Hipwood's shipyard which was on the left bank of the river immediately downstream of Westgate Bridge. In the top picture the ketch is under construction; Samuel Hipwood is on the right. In the bottom picture the ketch is about to be launched.

FLOODS OUTSIDE THE OLD CUSTOM HOUSE, 1947. Note the buildings further to the right. These were demolished before the building of the Quayside Wing of Shire Hall.

THE CONVICT SHIP *SUCCESS* in Gloucester Docks c.1908. The *Success* was never really a convict ship, she was built in Burma in about 1840 and was mainly employed in the Australian emigrant trade (voluntary not forced!) until 1852. She was then bought by the Australian State Government to house drunks and other troublesome characters. Her chequered career included a prison for deserting sailors and a coal hulk before eventually being brought to England. The convict exhibition was in effect a fairground type of act.

HORSE DRAWN WAGONS belonging to Priday Metford & Company for distribution of their flour c.1900.

GLOUCESTER DOCKS c.1880. These two pictures and the full sized picture opposite were all taken by the same photographer, probably on the same day. The reason why they were taken is not known, but they certainly give a flavour of what dock life was like at that time.

GLOUCESTER DOCKS C.1880. This fine photograph must be one of the best surviving views of the docks from the late nineteenth century.

The Revd. Francis Witts gives a good account of the opening in his diary for 1827.

April 26th.

This day was a great holiday in Gloucester. The Berkeley canal now fully completed, being opened. Two large vessels, with a considerable number of smaller ones, arrived in the afternoon in the canal basin, amid the greetings of many thousand spectators, having performed successfully the voyage from the basin at Sharpness Point. One of these ships was a three-master, a large square-rigged vessel, the other a brig. In the evening I saw them moored in the spacious basin, bedecked with flags and streamers, and refreshments lined the margin of the basin. The Canal Company has erected a very large range of warehouses contiguous, and provided that no impediment interferes from shifting sands in the Severn at the mouth of the canal, the great work now accomplished will be of infinite service to the city and this part of the country.

ALBERT MILLS IN GLOUCESTER DOCKS c.1880.

TWO VIEWS OF GLOUCESTER DOCKS. The bottom view looking towards the North Warehouse, now the headquarters of Gloucester City Council.

SPARTAN, GLOSTER. A detail of this picture is shown on page 13. The North Warehouse and the river lock are shown centre distant.

GLOUCESTER FROM THE WEST CHANNEL. This 1928 view shows the railway viaduct carrying the Gloucester to South Wales line. The line was opened as far as Chepstow in 1851, presumably the viaduct was built shortly before this, the embankments themselves having been formed with earth excavated from the canal dock construction, c.1848.

GLOUCESTER CATHEDRAL FROM THE EAST CHANNEL c.1900.

SECTION TWO

The City Streets

BULL LANE c.1890. The Midland Railway carrier wagon was a common sight around the city. The demise of railway carrier wagons is a recent phenomenom. Up until the 1970s British Railways took a vast proportion of the parcel business, now this is just a trickle compared to road carriers.

Bull Lane was greatly changed by the building of the telephone exchange on the left hand side in the 1930s, with extensions in the 1960s.

THE CROSS c.1905. The corner of Westgate Street and Northgate Street, showing H. Hargreaves, dispensing chemists shortly before it was demolished to make way for the Midland Bank.

THE CROSS c.1920. The corner of Northgate Street and Eastgate Street.

THE CROSS C.1905, looking from Westgate Street to Eastgate Street. St. Michael's was demolished in the 1950s, the tower alone remains and now serves as the Tourist Information Office.

THE CROSS, looking from Southgate Street to Northgate Street. The Photograph was used on a postcard sent in 1916 to a convalescent home in Yorkshire. The recipient had obviously been wounded on the Western Front, and this was a card with 'fond love' from his Nancy.

TWO VIEWS OF NORTHGATE STREET, looking towards the Cross. The top picture can be dated to c.1920, the bottom view is considerably earlier, probably c.1890. In the bottom picture note the original Bon Marché. The two-page spread on pages 32 and 33 dates from c.1910, the Bon Marche has a new 'north wing' by this date.

TWO VIEWS OF THE OXBODE, looking west. The top picture is late 1930s, the bottom one c.1959.

LOWER NORTHGATE STREET, the top picture c.1908. It is after 1904 because of the electric tram, but before 1910 because St. John's chuch still has all of its spire. The bottom picture is earlier, certainly before 1904 as two horse trams are evident. The first tram is coming out of Worcester Street, St. Peter's Roman Catholic church is in the distance.

BEFORE AND AFTER. Demolition at the junction of Worcester Street and Northgate Street in 1959 to make way for the new Lloyds Bank branch.

SOUTHGATE STREET AT THE CROSS, c.1906. The double page spread on pages 38 and 39 show Southgate street c.1922. I consider this to be one of the best pictures in the book - well deserving enlargement. The young pigeon-toed paperboy would be about 75 now. Does anyone know who he is?

THE BELL HOTEL, SOUTHGATE STREET c.1906. This is a coloured lithograph postcard taken from an original photograph. On the back of the postcard is written 'stayed here Tuesday night, 19 June'. According to my calculations this would make his stay either 1906 or 1912. I would think it was the earlier date.

THE BELL HOTEL c.1930.

45507. Gloucester, Southgate St. F.

Gloucester. Southgate Street H. L. Carter, Gloucester

TWO VIEWS OF SOUTHGATE STREET. The top picture can be dated to 1925 and shows the Ram Hotel, now the New County. The bottom picture is earlier, probably c.1908, and shows Southgate Street from the other direction, looking down towards Kimbrose Way.

The picture on pages 42 and 43 is probably c.1900. It is definitely prior to 1904 as the tram lines for the horse trams are still in existence. The view is taken looking south. The double page spread on pages 44 and 45 is looking towards the junction of Longsmith Street c.1930. Note the propensity of prams and their dimensions!

TWO VIEWS OF EASTGATE STREET LOOKING WEST. The top picture probably dates from c.1925, the bottom picture is earlier, c.1908.

TWO SPURS OFF EASTGATE STREET. Clarence Street shown above was decorated for Edward VII's visit to Gloucester in June 1909. The picture below shows the Spa Rooms at the junction of Brunswick Road and Spa Road. In 1814 springs were discovered whilst sinking a well, and this led to Gloucester's unsuccessful attempt to steal away some of the limelight from Cheltenham. The areas of Spa Road, Brunswick Road and Square, and Montpellier all date from c.1820 and the 'spa conspiracy'.

The picture on pages 48 and 49 show Eastgate Street prior to 1904, looking towards the Cross with the market visible on the left. The double page spread on pages 50 and 51 is taken from almost the same spot, except that this is 25 years later, and the photographer has stepped out into the road by eight feet or so.

EASTGATE MARKET in the late 1950s prior to demolition and relocation.

HURRAN & THOMAS at Eastgate Market.

BARTON GATES the demolition of Coles' shop, 26 April 1937, this picture shows the first lorry owned by J. Roman & Co. Ltd.

TWO VIEWS OF WESTGATE STREET TAKEN FROM THE CROSS. The top picture is c.1922, the bottom picture probably c.1908.

WESTGATE STREET c.1900. This fascinating picture shows the Theatre Royal on the right hand side, and what must have been the precursor to the cinema in Gloucester, a sign advertising 'Living Pictures', left of centre in our photograph.

The double page spread on pages 56 and 57 dates from c.1925, a bustling shopper looks around at the photographer as she proceeds with her marketing. Left of centre is F.W. Woolworth and four premises to the left is The Palladium.

The quality of the original photograph on page 58 tempted me to have a section enlarged. Unfortunately the background is rather dark, but caught by the camera is an errand boy, totally unaware that he was being photographed as he puzzles out his employer's delivery instructions on the parcel.

TWO VIEWS OF WESTGATE STREET. The top picture c.1915 showing that the Theatre Royal has turned into the Palace. The bottom picture is an actual photograph postcard dated May 1911. The picture was therefore taken some time earlier, probably 1910. It shows the Rose & Rose, two doors down from the Fleece.

LAYING THE TRAM LINES. Westgate Street, looking towards the Cross in 1904, the Rose & Rose is further up the street behind the workmen.

WESTGATE STREET c.1931. This photograph is looking east towards the Cross. Westgate Street was really the Shaftesbury Avenue of Gloucester, behind the Old Bear Inn is another theatre, just below the facade to Shire Hall, built in 1816 and retained during rebuilding this century.

COLLEGE STREET c.1925. College Street was much narrower until 1890 when all of the eastern side was demolished and the present buildings built in their place, some fifteen feet back from the original road frontage.

BERKELEY STREET IN THE LATE 1950S. This photograph was taken on an April afternoon in the late 1950s from Bearland House, then the headquarters of Post Office Telephones. The cathedral tower appears white, and very beautiful against a backdrop of a black thunder cloud. The bright sunlight creates a shadow of Bearland House on the headquarters of the County Library, demolished when the extension to the telephone exchange was built.

When the demolition occurred, a builder who had supervised the construction of the library actually cried, saying it was such a beautiful and perfectly constructed building, the like of which would never be seen again.

LOWER WESTGATE STREET c.1910

GLOUCESTER CATHEDRAL the Palace Yard c.1905. The building on the right is a late-fifteenth-century hall built on the site of the building in which Richard II held his parliament in 1378.

THE ONE-TIME CORNER of the Quay and Lower Westgate Street. Two businesses used the same entrance way, the Lower Westgate Street Post office, at No. 1, in the charge of the Gosney Family (c. 1897–1908), and, at No. 1a, Bunday's Coffee Tavern.

LITTLE CLOISTER C.1880. The boy shown here is delivering milk, he has his can of milk in his right hand, and the measuring pot in his left.

THE CATHEDRAL FROM THE RIVER C. 1880. This view was taken from the river bank, across Mean Ham to St. Oswald's Road. These cottages shown in the foreground are still standing, and bound onto the dual carriageway.

TUFFLEY AVENUE c.1900.

A ROW OF HOUSES AT CONEY HILL. This rather bleak picture was taken c.1900 and shows Coney Hill before the major housing developments.

A Tour of the Suburbs and Surrounding Villages

LUNCHEONS AND TEAS PROVIDED. The Churchdown tea gardens, Chapel Hay, c.1910. The hill is shown with surprisingly few trees, these have all grown around the church within the last eighty years.

CHAPEL HAY LANE c.1900.

THE OLD ELM AT CHURCHDOWN. This picture was taken c.1935 and shows the Old Elm shortly before its demolition. It stood on what is now the car park to the Bat and Ball, and the newly built Bat and Ball can be seen standing behind the Elm, rather dwarfing it. The photograph was taken from Chapel Hay.

RECHABITES AT CHURCHDOWN, 1908. The Independent Order of Rechabites were established on 25 August 1835; inspired by a Jewish sect of pastoral ascetics who flourished in the tenth century B.C.

MR. F.J. MERRETT the Churchdown blacksmith c.1910.

OUTSIDE THE VILLAGE FORGE, Mr. Merrett at Churchdown, c.1910.

THE OLD ELM INN at Churchdown. A happier picture than that on page 71, you can almost sense the sun shining before the cloud of the Bat and Ball. This picture c.1910.

THE OLD HOUSE AT HOME, Churchdown c.1900, a beer house until 1913.

LAND SLIP AT COOPER'S HILL. The construction of the Brockworth aircraft shadow factory during the late 1930s created thousands of tons of surplus soil and rubble which was dumped at Fidler's Elbow near Cooper's Hill. Storm water started a slippage of this soil which gradually moved down hill, threatening a farm which had to be evacuated. The story made national headlines and thousands of sightseers converged on the spot. In the bottom picture a barn has been virtually engulfed.

BARNWOOD COURT 1921. A complete series of photographs were taken of Barnwood Court in 1921, both interior and exterior. These two pictures show the front and side elevations.

INTERIOR AT BARNWOOD COURT. These two pictures from the 1921 series show the hall and conservatory with its laden vine, and magazines nonchalantly left on the folding table.

LATE SUMMER AT BARNWOOD COURT. Two more of the 1921 views. When a book such as this is being put together, a great deal of time has to be spent investigating detail in each picture to ascertain its date, or to find additional interest. In this 1921 series, the collective element is helpful in the detective work. The picture above has potted aspidisdra in the fireplace indicating that it is summer, and on the previous page the size of the grapes on the vine indicate late August, early September. If we had not known that it was 1921, a further clue indicating circa First World War would be the photograph on the occasional table.

THE CROSS HANDS, BROCKWORTH. The top photograph looking towards Cheltenham was taken in 1922. The bottom picture looking towards Cooper's Hill is three years later.

HUCCLECOTE GREEN in the 1920s. In Samuel Rudder's *New History of Gloucestershire* published in 1779, Rudder says the name Hucclecote derives from the Celtic 'Ukel' meaning high, and 'Coed' meaning wood. The more scientific analysis by the English Place Name Society says that the derivation is 'Huccla's Cottage'. In Domesday (1086) it is referred to as Hochlicote.

HUCCLECOTE and the junction to Churchdown Lane 1959.

UNKNOWN HOUSE, possibly at Matson. One of the sources for this book was a fine album of photographs with little or no information. Perhaps a reader could advise on the actual house, location and approximate date, so that the correct detail may be added in a subsequent edition of this book.

ROBINSWOOD HILL a view from c.1910.

THE WIDENING OF BARNWOOD ROAD and the rebuilding of the railway bridge 1936.

HURRAN'S NURSERY, the original Churchdown premises of Alfred Hurran.

COLEBRIDGE HOUSE, LONGLEVENS. Two views of Colebridge House as it was c.1920. The house was demolished in the 1930s to make way for housing estates. The Double Gloucester now stands on the site.

TWO VIEWS OF LONGLEVENS in the 1930s. The top photograph is of Cheltenham Road looking north with the junction to Elmbridge Road on the immediate right. The picture must have been taken some time prior to 1938 as the shop on the right is shown to be run by Mr. F.C. Mortimer, who was sub-postmaster until that time. The new Cheltenham Road was opened in 1926. The old road went to the left of Anderson's Garage, shown left in the photograph. The bottom picture shows Oxtall's Road, not long after the houses had been built.

HAYMAKING AT SNEEDHAMS GREEN. The date is unspecified, but possibly c. 1945.

ELM TREES AT BROOKTHORPE c. 1930. The trees were planted to celebrate the victory at Waterloo, but fell victim to old age and were felled long before Dutch Elm Disease did its work in the rest of the county. These trees were replaced by chestnut trees which are all now mature.

THE KING'S HEAD, NORTON c. 1905. The pub is now considerably altered from this Edwardian view. The front has now been rendered, and apart from the many alterations outside, the interior has been ripped out to make a modern public house instead of the 'parlour', the 'smoke', the 'snug' and the 'bar'.

UNIDENTIFIED FARMHOUSE AROUND GLOUCESTER. This fine photograph comes from the same album of local views mentioned on page 80. If anyone knows where this house is, or was, please write in so that correct information may be given in subsequent editions of this book.

PLEASURE FARM, LONGFORD C. 1910. The farm was used as a transport depot for many years, the house was demolished several years ago to make way for housing development.

SUTTON'S MILL, CRANHAM C. 1850. This picture is without doubt the earliest view shown in this book. It may even have been taken by W.H. Fox-Talbot, the pioneer of photography who came from Lacock Abbey in Wiltshire. The miller also came from the village of Lacock. Note the churchwarden clay pipes.

Pubs, Shops and Garages

THE NEW INN C. 1905. Amongst postcard dealers' collections, this view of the New Inn is the most common. There are many variations, but they are invariably taken from the same spot showing the stairs and gallery. Note the postman on the right-hand side.

THE MONKS' RETREAT C. 1910. It was supposed that this underground vault beneath the Fleece was constructed by Benedictine monks in the twelth century and at one time to have been connected by a tunnel, part of which remains, to St. Peter's Abbey which is now the cathedral. The truth of this I do not know, I merely repeat this often told anecdote. According to more recent (and more reputable authorities), the undercroft was indeed twelfth-century, but nothing more romantic than a wealthy man's cellar!

THE RAM & COUNTY HOTEL C. 1915. The Ram & County is now the New County Hotel. The cars outside are early model 'T' Fords.

THE LEMON AND PARKER c. 1902. This photograph was lent by Mr. A. Watts, whose father shown on the left aged 21 was manager for 44 years. The Lemon and Parker was closed in the early 1970s, and the building is now Town Books and Toys.

THE THREE COCKS INN c. 1880.

SALLY URSELL'S SWEET SHOP in Barton Street, c. 1905. Sally Ursell (shown on the right) ran the shop and made ice cream on the premises until 1933 when her niece Gertrude Norris took over.

A PRE-WAR CHEMIST'S SHOP. These two pictures are unfortunately not in Gloucester, but they show, on the left, a Gloucestrian, Mr. L.E. Copeland who took several of the pictures used in this book. He was a relief dispenser for Messrs. Hedges Ltd. of Birmingham for a few years before the war, this shop being the Balsall Heath branch, where they are trying on their recently issued gas masks. Chamberlain's Munich accord had been signed with Hitler on 30 September 1938; these photographs were taken 11 November 1938.

TINGLE'S CHRISTMAS. The Christmas show of meat and dressed poultry in 1938. On the left is Ted Tingle, and on the right Archie Jaynes. The shop was at 78 Barton Street.

F. WILLIAMS' GROCERY C. 1926 The shop was in Westgate Street; Mrs. Williams and children pose for the camera.

THE BUILDING OF MARKS & SPENCER in Northgate Street in the early 1930s. It is interesting to see that the use of superlatives such as 'New Super Store' is nothing new!

MR. A WILLIAMSON, GENERAL DEALER in Hare Lane c. 1920.

H.E. JONES, PHOTOGRAPHER in Northgate Street c. 1906. Jones' shop was on the west side of the street, the site now being covered by Sainsbury's. Many of the early photographs in this book were postcard views by Jones, probably the major photographer in the city at the time.

Gloucester, Bishop Hooper's House.

BISHOP HOOPER PHARMACY C. 1900. This building in Westgate Street now houses the Folk Museum.

TWO VIEWS OF KING'S SQUARE and the Oxebode, a few years after the building of the Bon Marché in 1930. The St. Aldate Garage site is clearly seen.

AN EARLY VIEW OF ST. ALDATE GARAGE C. 1931. The age of the cars would tempt an earlier date, but they are presumably second-hand. Mitre Street, which became the Oxbode shows signs of demolition.

THE NEW ST. ALDATE GARAGE in 1947, with Hermann Goering's Mercedes Benz on display as a promotion.

THE CITY GARAGE in Worcester Street c. 1910.

FRED NORRIS'S GARAGE in Market Parade c. 1908.

Gloucester
at War

ON THE WESTERN FRONT in 1915. Trooper Hubert Barnes (nearest camera) is looking at a picture of his fiancée, Clementine. He came home to Gloucester on leave on 19 December, and he and Clementine were married on the 21st. After that he had to wait for eighteen months before he saw his wife again! His next home leave not occurring until July 1917.

BOYS PLAYING SOLDIERS in Bishopstone Road, 1914.

'PRIVATE' BRIAN MAPES outside Post 'A' Head
Warden, 25 Victoria Street c. 1940.

LOCAL DEFENCE VOLUNTEERS on Sunday 19 May 1940 at Kingsholm.
Below, the LDV near Twigworth School on the way to church parade at Twigworth Church, August 1940.

THE HOME GUARD at Sneedham's Green, 28 March 1942. All of 'B' Company on Field Day. This picture is of No. 2 Section, 7 Platoon, B Company. Sergeant Rawson, Section Commander for Sandhurst.

COLLECTING SCRAP FOR SPITFIRES. Part of the wartime propaganda in 1940 was collecting scrap for the war effort – the popular theme was that it was for building Spitfires, although in reality this was far from the truth. Although the metal was very useful, the real purpose behind the excercise was morale boosting following the debacle with the B.E.F. and the evacuation from Dunkirk. The collection here was at Parry Hall, Tredworth, 1940.

WARDENS ON PARADE. The Gloucester Wardens marching to the cathedral, Mr. G. Mapes in the centre, wearing his three medals from the First World War.

HEAD WARDEN'S POST, Victoria Street. From left to right; Olive Stephens, Mr. Niland, Mr. Smith, Mr. Crimps and Mr. G. Mapes.

WARTIME DANCE at Fielding and Platt.

A WARTIME SOCIAL EVENING Held at the Guildhall, Eastgate Street.

THE CITIZEN FUND, 1940. Cigarette issue from the Citizen fund at the Drill Hall.

A PRE-WAR ARMY DISPLAY. Eastgate Street, October 1936.

GLOSTER GORAL J8673. This is not a wartime picture, but as most of the G.A.C. pictures following are related to the Second World War, this seemed the logical section to include it. The Gloster Aircraft Company was a major employer in Gloucester up to the early 1960s, and although the aircraft manufacturing has gone, there is still one legacy at the Brockworth site, and that is Gloster Saro, still a Hawker Siddeley company – Phoenix out of the ashes! The aircraft shown above was built at Gloucester and had its first flight in February 1927. It was a development aircraft, and only this one was ever built.

PILOT TRAINING AT STAVERTON 1939. Airwork Limited trained pilots at Staverton for the R.A.F. V.R., most training being carried out with Tiger Moths, although Gloster Gladiators were also stationed there.

111

GLOSTER TC.33. 4 Rolls Royce Kestrel engines powered this G.A.C. bomber, the largest aeroplane built at Gloucester and first demonstrated in 1931. Again, only one was ever built.

GLOSTER GAMECOCK G-EBNT. This particular aeroplane was G.A.C.'s company demonstrator. This picture was taken in 1926.

HURRICANE PRODUCTION AT BROCKWORTH. King George VI and Queen Elizabeth visiting G.A.C. in 1940 during the peak of Hawker Hurricane production. In the bottom picture, the General Manager, Frank McKenna is shown to our left of the Queen.

BROCKWORTH FROM THE AIR, a 1942 overhead view of G.A.C. showing aircraft on the ground below the camouflaged factory.

STAVERTON FROM THE AIR, a 1939 picture of the newly built Staverton, taken from a Gloster Gladiator.

THE LAST TYPHOON. 1945, and the end of the war. The last Typhoon rolls out of the factory amid bunting and flags. The top picture was taken in November 1945 and includes some of the G.A.C. staff.

ARMY CADETS ON PARADE in Gloucester Park, 1944.

A GLOSTER GLADIATOR at Staverton, 1939.

V.E. DAY, 9 MAY 1945. Two street parties in Gloucester. The top picture is in Vauxhall Road, the bottom one in Clare Street.

THE 1947 FLOODS. As if the misery of the Second World War had not been enough, fate handed out one of the worst winters on record in 1946–7. Coal stocks throughout the country were still low after the war, and the severe weather created a huge demand for fuel which could not be moved even if some stock were available! Many weeks of heavy snowfalls and frosts suddenly broke in March, and the melting snow created more misery with flooding throughout the country. These two photographs were taken 22 March 1947 and show Dean's Walk and St. Oswald's Road under several feet of water.

TWO GLOSTER METEORS side by side in the colours of the Egyptian Air Force prior to delivery in the early 1950s. They are flying over Morelands Match Factory and the Wagon Works, the Bristol Road being between the two factories. The streets to the left of the match factory are (right to left), Philip Street, Robin Hood Street, Theresa Street, Alma Place, Clegram Road, Frampton Road and Lysons Avenue. Baker's Quay is plainly visible on the canal, and the river Severn is seen in the distance behind Hempsted.

Schools and Sports

LINDEN ROAD INFANTS in 1915.

ST. MARY DE CRYPT CRICKETERS, 1910. Mr. A.C. Perry is shown centre bat in the front row as he was aged 10.

ST. ALDATE'S BIBLE CLASS OF 1898.

PUPILS AT BROCKWORTH SCHOOL.

TWO GROUPS AT HARTPURY CHURCH OF ENGLAND SCHOOL. The top group seen in 1926 are from left to right, back row: Miss Nolan, teacher; — ; Pat Diamond; — ; Jack Harris; Hubert Whyat; Jim Diamond; Jack Woodcock; Mr. Dance, headmaster. Middle row: — ; — ; Muriel Banks; Gertrude Browett; Betty Woodcock; Phyllis Banks. Front row: Joan Dance; Elsie Hiam; — ; Eunice Davis; Kathleen Banks and Kathleen Lake.

Some of the same children are shown in this picture of three years later. Back row: Daisy Stanton; Jim Andrews; Stan Vaughan; 'Tichy' Howells. Centre row: Jim Diamond; Gertrude Browett; Victor Price; Hedley Jones; Winnie Parsons; Alice Forty; Frank Lambrett; Charlie Smart; and Jack Woodcock. Front row: Phyllis Banks; Elsie Hiam; Dorothy Banks; Mollie Lambrett; Joan Dance; Betty Woodcock and Kathleen Lake.

RYECROFT SCHOOL in the first decade of this century.

THE LAST PUPILS at Brockworth National School, February 1960.

SIR THOMAS RICH'S SCHOOL c. 1880. Sir Thomas endowed his first school in 1666. The school pictured here was built in 1807, and demolished shortly before 1890 to make way for the new guildhall.

ST. PETER'S ROMAN CATHOLIC SCHOOL c. 1915.

DENMARK ROAD SCHOOL c. 1905.

OLD HOUSE St. Catherine Street, in which Robert Raikes held the first Sunday School in England in 1781. This photograph was taken c. 1900.

THE FIRST GIRLS SUNDAY SCHOOL founded by Robert Raikes a few years after the boys school. This photograph c. 1900.

THE GIRL'S HIGH SCHOOL c.1905. This school, previously called the Endowed School was at Bearland House (see page 63).

GLOUCESTER JUNIOR TECHNICAL COLLEGE FIRST ELEVEN 1945–46. This team retained an unbeaten record throughout the season. From left to right, back row: B.J.G. Brooks; J.W. Proctor; R.W. Morse; D. Merritt; E.C. Davis; D. Phillbrick; B. Cockburn; J. Davis and L.T. Longney. Front row: Mr. P.B. Balcock; P.H.L. Summers; P.R. Baker; Dr. Watson (principal); G.D. White; T.P. Greening and Mr. J. Walker.

GLOUCESTER WOTTON TENNIS CLUB c. 1881. The house in the background still exists, although in a modernised form. The pavilion to the left was burned down in the late 1940s. The club is still going strong, over a hundred years after this picture was taken. The exact date of foundation is unknown.

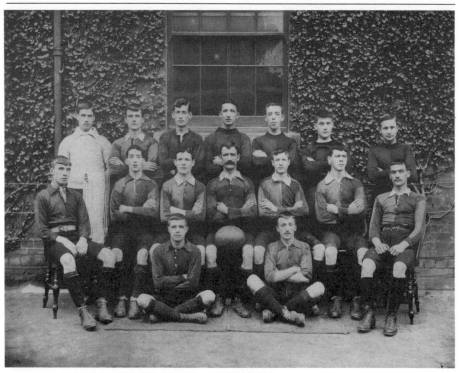

GORDON WANDERERS 'A' RUGBY FOOTBALL TEAM 1901–2 season.
From left to right, back row: C. Pallister; T. Pallister; A. Strainge; H. Taylor; A. Pegler; B. Beecham and F. Bayliss. Middle row: H. Chapman; T. Stephens; F. Stephens; J.W. Ford; J. Mayhew; S. Bailey and W. Langford. Front row: A. Harris and A. Overthrow.

MORELAND'S RUGBY FOOTBALL CLUB 1905–6 season.
From left to right, back row: W. Hancock; A. Strain; E. Pegler; G. Underwood; G. Phelps; T. Bailey; G. Hale and W. Boyce. Third row: J. Kibble; J. Lewis; W.H. Rodway; H. Moulsdale; S. Brazer; T. Toomey; J. Price; J. Ible; H. While; H. Lapworth; C. Lane and H. Bayliss. Second row: H. Langford; W.J. Slatter; T. Bagwell; D. Bretherton; W. Landford; F. Ewers; P. Hancock; G. Austin and J. Barradine. Front: F. Bullock and W. Rigby.

Road and Rail

BRITISH ROAD SERVICES India Road Depot, some time after 1948. Clement Attlee's post-war Labour government set about a programme of nationalization, the turn of road services came in 1948 when all haulage companies above a certain size were incorporated into the new British Road Services.

A MORE SEDATE MODE OF TRANSPORT, Highnam Corner c.1900

STYLE IN CLARENCE STREET. Dr. Edgar Ellis' chauffeur, Richard Lyman c. 1908. Note the very early number plate.

SYMONDS' HORSE BUSES c. 1895. The Symonds horse buses competed with the horse trams. George Symonds' 'cab, omnibus and funeral establishment' was in Worcester Street. The shadow between the two buses on the right is the old railway bridge over Worcester Street, replaced in 1902.

EMERGENCY VEHICLES AT STAVERTON AIRPORT in 1939.

CHANGING ENDS, changing the horse to the other end of a horse tram c. 1900. The view is in Southgate Street.

POLING THE 'PICK-UP' in 1932. In a similar fashion to the horse trams, the electric trams needed to have their electricity pick-up conductor changed over at each terminus point. This one is at Bristol Road. The tram is in grey livery.

TWO TRAMS AT THE STROUD ROAD TERMINUS C.1908. The left-hand one shows its destination as 'Kingsholm via Stroud Road' (i.e. via Sudbrook); the other is 'Cross' (via Park End Road).

A TRAM AT BARNWOOD ROAD at the junction of Elmbridge Road, C.1906.

CORPORATION TRAMCAR AT WESTGATE BRIDGE *c.* 1905. This is a delightful picture that must have given its owner great pleasure in capturing.

A CRASH AT LOWER BARTON STREET in 1918.

CITY OF TRURO at Gloucester 18 May 1957.

STAFF AT EASTGATE STATION c. 1925. This was the L.M.S. (London, Midland and Scottish Railway) station, the site of which is now covered by Asda and the Anglo-American Insurance Building. The other Gloucester station, Central Station, stood on the site of the current British Rail station and was operated by the Great Western Railway.

JOE HARRINGTON OUTSIDE HIS SIGNALBOX c. 1920. This box was at Sudbrook Crossing, Southgate Street, on the Midland Railway, High Orchard Street branch line to the docks. The line followed the line of the new road from Southgate Street through the park to Park End Road, and joined up with the Midland line which originally ran parallel to Stroud Road, curving around adjacent to Park End Road, through what is now the B & Q DIY Superstore, across Barton Street at the cross-roads immediately below All Saints Church, leading into the L.M.S. station.

Joe Harrington joined the Midland Railway in 1900, and worked there all his life, retiring in 1950.

ACHILLES AT GLOUCESTER c. 1900. Number 3031, Achilles, built in 1894, was the first of the Achilles class. Designed by William Dean with 7 foot 8 inch driving wheels, cylinder 19 inches in diameter with 24 inch stroke and a working pressure of 160 pounds per square inch; weight in running order, 49 tons. Fifty of the class were built between 1894 and 1899. The Achilles class was the mainstay of the G.W.R. express services until the increasing weight of the trains, with the introduction of dining cars and new coaches proved beyond them. The last of the class was withdrawn and scrapped in 1915.

GLOUCESTER MIDLAND STATION, later known as Eastgate, shown as it was between 1896, when it was opened, and about 1906 when the style of locomotive painting began to change. This view is from a contemporary postcard.

AN AERIAL VIEW OF GLOUCESTER illustrating the route of the L.M.S. line along Park End Road (see caption on page 142). The church by the park is the United Reformed Church in Park Road. This view of c. 1935 shows the vast extent of the former railway complex at Gloucester. The Barton Street signal box straddles the line immediately to our left of All Saints Church, and the line then runs into Eastgate Station. The line then curves away towards Barnwood and then to Churchdown and Cheltenham; the lines meet up with those running out of the G.W.R. 'Central Station'. The long footbridge in the centre joined the two stations.

Institutions

THE INFIRMARY C. 1900. The Infirmary was purpose built as a hospital in 1755, largely through the efforts of Lord Botetourt and the Revd. Talbot. The hospital was originally funded from voluntary subscriptions and hospital 'clubs'. It was renamed the Gloucester Royal Hospital in 1909 during the visit of Edward VII. It was made redundant by the building of the new hospital in Great Western Road, and was finally demolished in 1985. A sad end to what could have been a finely restored building.

SMALLPOX ISOLATION HOSPITAL at Longlevens, c. 1896. Edward Jenner conceived and developed vaccination in 1796 at Berkeley, just twenty miles south of Gloucester. In Great Britain vaccination was made compulsory in 1853, but even so, lapses in the vaccination programme during the 1880s had disastrous consequences during the smallpox epidemic of 1895–96.

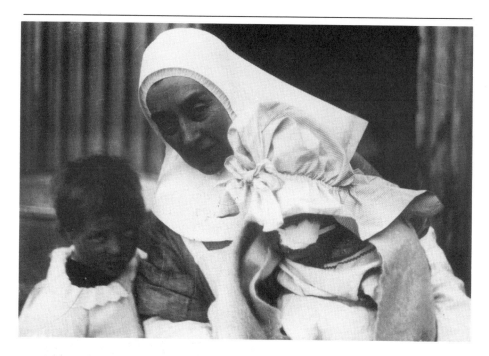

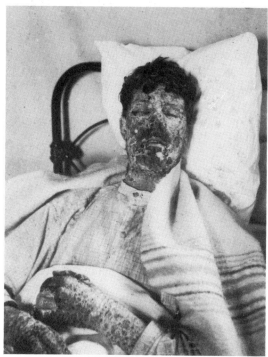

Above: Children at the smallpox isolation hospital. Below: Edwin Davis of 9 Lower Barton Street, an example of how terrible smallpox could be on patients who actually survived. The facial scourging left vast pox marks, and in some cases virtually destroyed faces. Smallpox eradication was achieved throughout the world in the 1970s, a success story for the World Health Organization. If, for that one success alone, well justifies the existence of the United Nations Organization together with its sub-agencies.

GLOUCESTER PRISON C. 1900. The prison was built in 1792 along the lines advocated by the prison reformer John Howard. In Gloucestershire, much of the agitation for reform came from Sir George Onesiphorus Paul; a one time gambler and dilettante who abandoned his irresponsible life, and dedicated his life to the improvement of prisons in Gloucestershire.

ST. BARTHOLOMEW'S HOSPITAL Westgate Street c. 1960. The hospital was founded in the twelfth century, but nearly all of the earlier building was destroyed in the construction of the almshouses in 1786.

THE PUBLIC LIBRARY, BRUNSWICK ROAD shortly after its opening in 1900.

SECTION NINE

Events

BARTON FAIR MARKET, C. 1905. An Act of Parliament was passed in 1821 enabling a separate market to take place away from the actual Barton Fair held in the street on 28 September annually. Market buildings were erected on what is now the bus station in 1855, these were replaced or enlarged in a building programme of 1897–8.

BARTON FAIR in Eastgate Street, 1882.

ALL SAINTS MOTHERS UNION in 1900.

VINEGAR WORKS OUTING TO SYMOND'S YAT 26 July 1923.

OFF TO CAMP c. 1923. Members of the British Boy Scouts, who were attached to the Wesley Hall in Seymour Road, about to set off for their annual camp at Birtsmorton, near Malvern. The vehicle is a Thorneycroft lorry (probably army surplus after the First World War) belonging to Hough and Whitmore. Note the solid tyres – this must have been a hard ride.

GLOUCESTER CO-OP CHORAL SOCIETY Christmas show c. 1943. Held at Tyndale Church Hall, Stratton Road.

CORONATION FESTIVITIES IN UNION STREET 1953.

FIRE AT ALL SAINTS CHURCH c.1895.

ALCOHOL IS POISON! A temperance march entering Worcester Street from Northgate Street c. 1900. The front banner seems to read 'Alcohol is Poison'. Note the Symonds horse bus, above the name 'Pioneer' is the destination board, reading 'Longford Twigworth Norton'. I wonder if the marchers noticed? The horse tram at the end of the procession is advertising Godsell's Ales.

ACKNOWLEDGEMENTS

I would like to thank all those listed below who have made the compilation of this book a pleasure. Nearly all of those approached for photographs not only willingly lent pictures included in this book, but also suggested additional sources, mentioned interesting anecdotes and showed genuine interest in the production of the book. Unfortunately only a part of the material could be used, but there is obvious scope for follow-up volumes.

My special thanks go to Mr. L.E. Copeland who lent pictures from his extensive collection – many of which were photographs he took in the 1930s and 1940s. The County Archivist and staff at Gloucestershire Record Office helped 'above and beyond the call of duty!' For individual contributions I wish to thank Mrs. B.G. Adams, Mrs. Peggy Alberts, Mrs. G. Bailey, Mr. S.G. Ballinger, Mrs. C. Barnes, Mr. H. Bayliss, Mrs. J.E. Belcher, Mr. N.F. Betteridge, Mrs. Betty Bevan, Mr. & Mrs. E.R. Bishop, Mr. Hubert William Boucher, Mr. Ken Brindley, Mr. Kenneth V. Browne, Mrs. E.V. Carter, Mrs. Gay Clark, Mrs. M. Coale, Mr. E. Currier L.R.P.S., Mrs. Joan Ellis, Mr. C. Etherington, Mr. R. Fletcher, Mrs. Mary M. Foylan, Mr. C. Franklin, Gloucester Wotton Tennis Club, Mrs. Mary Gough, Mrs. Ruth Hall, Mr. Charles H. Hampton, Mr. A.J. Hayward, Mr. A.V. Hazard, Mrs. Rosemary Hellerman, Mrs. S.J. Hickman, Mr. F. Holland, Mr. H. Household, Mr. A. Hurran, Mrs. U. Johnstone, Mr. S. Knight, Mr. F.G. Mann, Mrs. Jennie Marriott, Mr. F. Matthews, Mrs. G.M. Nunan, Mr. J. Peart, Mrs. H.N. Preece, Mr. E.V. Presley, Mr. J.W. Procter, Miss P.A. Rawson, Mrs. P. Roles, Mr. F.W. Rowbotham, Mr. A.E. Sheppard, Miss I.S. Starr, Mrs. J.C. Tingle, Mr. E.G. Watson, Mr. A. Watts, Mr. Jerry Williams, Miss Vera Wintle, Mr Ken Wixey, The Ken Wixey Collection and finally Mr. Jack Woodcock.

For reading my work and checking that I had not made any embarrassing mistakes I wish to thank Jill Voyce, and also her staff in the City Library who always offer such marvellous service. Finally, I thank my secretary, Theresa, who co-ordinated the loan of photographs in an amazingly efficient manner.

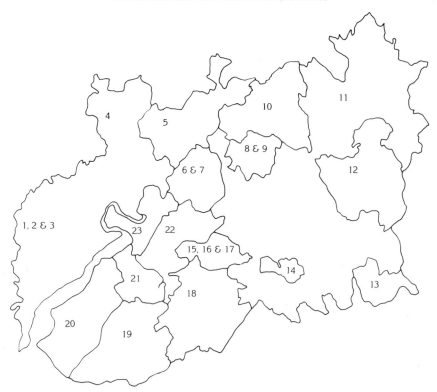